Earth's

by Carol Levine

PEARSON
Scott
Foresman

DK

How does Earth move?

Earth Seems to Stand Still

Earth is moving steadily and smoothly all the time. You cannot feel it because you are moving with it! You move at the same speed as the part of Earth you are on.

How can you tell Earth is moving? One way you can tell is by looking at the sky. The Sun and stars seem to move across the sky. They seem to move because Earth is turning.

Another way you can tell that Earth is turning is by the change in seasons. Some places on Earth have dramatic changes in season. These changes are not as easy to notice in other places. Changes in season are caused in part by how Earth moves through space.

Scientists have learned a lot about stars since people began studying the sky thousands of years ago. Tools such as telescopes, cameras, and computers help them study Earth's movement.

Earth's Rotation

A merry-go-round spins around a post in its center. Earth spins around an imaginary line that goes through its center. This line goes from the North Pole to the South Pole. It is Earth's **axis.**

The spinning of Earth around its axis is its **rotation.** One rotation of Earth is one full turn around its axis. One rotation of Earth takes almost 24 hours. Earth rotates from west to east. This makes objects in the sky appear to move from east to west.

Earth spins from west to east around its axis.

Why Shadows Change

A shadow appears when light shines on an object but cannot pass through it. Earth's rotation causes the Sun to shine on objects from different angles at different times of day. Earth's rotation also causes the change from night to day and day to night.

Daylight Hours

How do the number of daylight hours change during the year? Look at the chart below to see the data for a city in the Northern Hemisphere.

A short shadow appears around noon when the Sun seems high in the sky. Shadows are longer in the morning and evening.

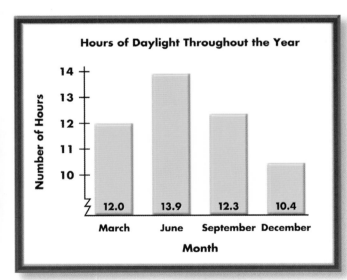

Hours of Daylight Throughout the Year

	March	June	September	December
Number of Hours	12.0	13.9	12.3	10.4

Month

Earth's Revolution

Earth travels around the Sun as it rotates. The path Earth takes around the Sun is its **orbit.** A **revolution** is the movement of one object around another. One revolution of Earth is one complete orbit around the Sun. One revolution takes about 365 days, or one year. Earth travels about 940,000,000 kilometers during one revolution. Earth's speed is about 107,000 kilometers per hour.

The shape of Earth's orbit is an **ellipse,** or a stretched-out circle. Earth is closer to the Sun in some parts of its orbit. It is farther from the Sun in others.

Earth would fly off into space if gravity did not pull it toward the Sun. If Earth did not keep moving, the attraction between Earth and the Sun would cause them to crash.

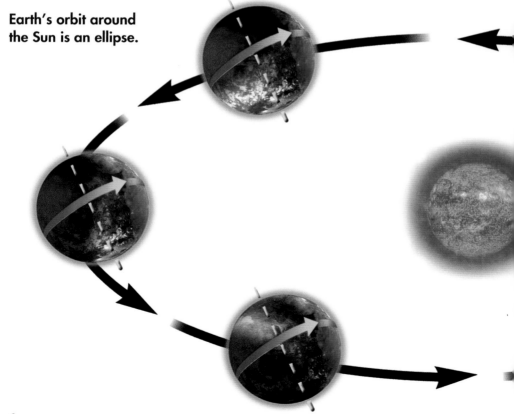

Earth's orbit around the Sun is an ellipse.

6

Earth's Tilted Axis

Earth's axis is always tilted in the same direction. One end of the axis is always tilted toward the North Star. This tilt causes different places on Earth to face the Sun directly at different parts of the orbit.

When the Northern Hemisphere is tilted toward the Sun, the Southern Hemisphere is tilted away from it. The Northern Hemisphere has summer. Daylight is longer than night. More direct sunlight means temperatures are higher. At the same time, it is winter in the Southern Hemisphere. Daylight is shorter and the temperatures are lower. When the Southern Hemisphere is tilted toward the Sun, it is summer there.

In spring and fall, the number of daylight and night hours is almost the same. Temperatures are neither very hot or cold.

When the North Pole is tilted toward the Sun, the Northern Hemisphere gets the most direct sunlight.

What patterns can you see in the sky?

Sun, Moon, and Earth

Sometimes the Moon can be seen at night. Sometimes the Moon can even be seen in the daytime. The Moon seems to shine. But it does not make its own light. Sunlight reflects off the surface of the Moon.

The Moon revolves around Earth. Its orbit is an ellipse. Gravity between Earth and the Moon keeps the Moon in its orbit. The Moon revolves around Earth in about 27 days.

The Moon also rotates around its axis. Each time it rotates one time on its axis, it also revolves one time around Earth. This causes the same side of the Moon to face Earth at all times. You can see only one side of the Moon from Earth.

The Phases of the Moon

The shape of the Moon seems to change at different times of the month. These shapes are called the phases of the Moon.

Light from the Sun reflects off the surface of half of the Moon. When that half faces Earth, the Moon looks like a full circle of light. This is called a full Moon. When the Moon's dark, unlighted side faces Earth, the Moon cannot be seen from Earth. This is called a new Moon.

A crescent Moon is a sliver of lighted Moon. The first quarter is half of the lighted half we can see on Earth, or one quarter of the Moon. The last quarter is also half of the lighted half of the Moon. This happens after a full Moon. Soon a new Moon will begin a new set of phases.

Crescent

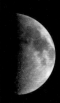

First quarter

Full Moon

Last quarter

Waning crescent

Eclipses

An **eclipse** happens when one object in space comes between the Sun and another object and casts its shadow on the other object. This takes place when the Moon passes through Earth's shadow, and when the Moon's shadow falls on Earth.

Light from the Sun allows us to see the Moon. But during some full moons, the Moon and the Sun are on opposite sides of Earth. That means Earth is between the Sun and the Moon. The Moon will usually move above or below Earth's shadow. But a **lunar eclipse** happens when the Moon passes through Earth's shadow.

Sometimes only part of the Moon crosses Earth's shadow during an eclipse. This makes the Moon look as if something took a bite from it. This is called a partial eclipse. A total lunar eclipse happens when the entire Moon is in Earth's shadow.

A lunar eclipse may last 100 minutes. Several lunar eclipses can take place each year.

Light from the Sun

During a lunar eclipse, Earth is between the Moon and the Sun. The Moon is in Earth's shadow.

Solar Eclipses

When the Moon passes between the Sun and Earth, it casts its shadow on Earth. This is a **solar eclipse.** The Moon's shadow covers only a part of Earth. The solar eclipse can be seen only from places on Earth where the Moon's shadow falls.

There can be solar eclipses two to five times each year. Total solar eclipses can last as long as 7.5 minutes. A solar eclipse can make the day seem as dark as night.

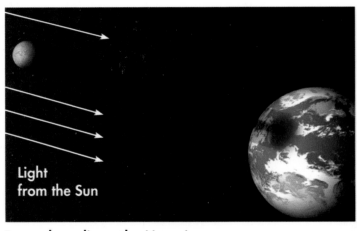

Light from the Sun

In a solar eclipse, the Moon is between Earth and the Sun. The Moon casts a shadow on Earth.

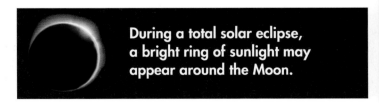

During a total solar eclipse, a bright ring of sunlight may appear around the Moon.

Viewing a Solar Eclipse Safely

It is very dangerous to look directly at the Sun. It is even dangerous during an eclipse. It is not safe to look right at the Sun using binoculars, sunglasses, smoked glass, exposed film, or a telescope. The Sun can cause permanent damage to your eyes. It can even cause blindness.

You can see a solar eclipse safely by watching the Sun's image on a screen. Sit or stand with the Sun behind you. Make a small hole in a sheet of paper or thin cardboard. Hold it in front of you. Put a second sheet of paper or cardboard behind the first one. You will see an image of the eclipse on the second sheet as the sunlight passes through the hole in the first sheet.

You can watch a solar eclipse safely by projecting its image through a telescope onto a sheet of paper.

Stars

Scientists believe that there are 1 billion trillion stars in the universe. That number is a 1 followed by 21 zeroes! For Earth, the Sun is the nearest and most important star. Living things need its energy and light. The Sun is an ordinary star. Like all stars, the Sun is a hot ball of gas. Some stars are bigger, brighter, or hotter. Many others are smaller, dimmer, and cooler.

The bright light of the Sun keeps us from seeing other stars in the daytime. City lights and cloudy weather can make stars hard to see at night in some places. The light from stars that are very far away may seem dim. Some stars are so far away that they can only be seen with a telescope.

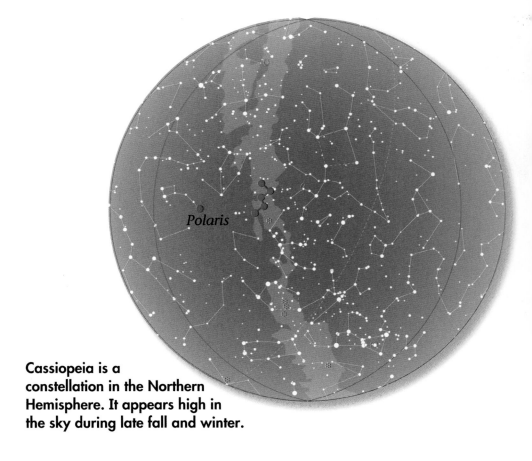

Polaris

Cassiopeia is a constellation in the Northern Hemisphere. It appears high in the sky during late fall and winter.

Star Patterns

A **constellation** is a pattern of stars. Stars are often identified by the constellation they are in. Stars in the same constellation may not be close to each other.

Stars seem to move across the sky as Earth rotates. They seem to move in straight lines at the equator. They seem to move in circles at the poles. Constellations seen in the Southern Hemisphere are different from those seen in the Northern Hemisphere.

The North Star, or Polaris, appears in the sky above the North Pole. The constellation Cassiopeia is near Polaris. Its position changes during the year.

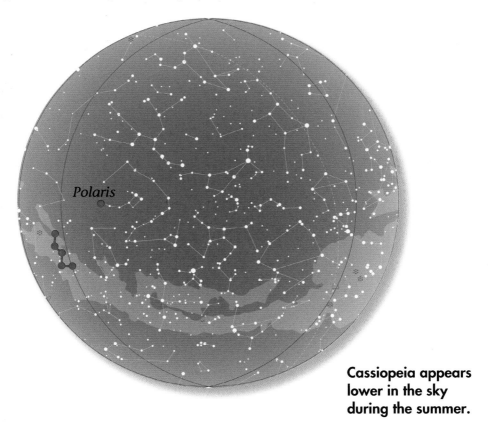

Polaris

Cassiopeia appears lower in the sky during the summer.

Glossary

axis   an imaginary line passing from the North Pole through the center of Earth to the South Pole

constellation   a pattern of stars in an area of the sky

eclipse   the passing of an object in space between the Sun and another object, causing a shadow to be cast on the other object

ellipse   a stretched-out circle

lunar eclipse   the passing of Earth between the Moon and the Sun, causing Earth's shadow to be cast on the Moon

orbit   the path an object takes around another object

revolution   the movement of one object around another

rotation   the spinning of an object around an axis

solar eclipse   the passing of the Moon between the Sun and Earth, causing the Moon's shadow to be cast on Earth